COOL CAREERS WITHOUT COLLEGE

CAREERS FOR PEOPLE WHO LOVE THE GREAT OUTDOORS

Siyavush Saidian

ROSEN
PUBLISHING

New York

Published in 2021 by The Rosen Publishing Group, Inc.
29 East 21st Street, New York, NY 10010

Copyright © 2021 by The Rosen Publishing Group, Inc.

First Edition

Portions of this work were originally authored by Sarah Machajewski and published as *Cool Careers Without College for People Who Love Nature*. All new material in this edition authored by Siyavush Saidian.

Library of Congress Cataloging-in-Publication Data

Names: Saidian, Siyavush.
Title: Careers for people who love the great outdoors / Siyavush Saidian.
Description: New York : Rosen Publishing, 2021. | Series: Cool careers without college | Includes bibliographical references and index.
Identifiers: ISBN 9781499468823 (pbk.) | ISBN 9781499468830 (library bound)
Subjects: LCSH: Outdoor life--Vocational guidance--Juvenile literature.
| Agriculture--Vocational guidance--Juvenile literature.
Classification: LCC HF5381.2 S24 2021 | DDC 331.702--dc23

Some of the images in this book illustrate individuals who are models. The depictions do not imply actual situations or events.

Manufactured in the United States of America

CONTENTS

INTRODUCTION

I n the hustle and bustle of the 21st-century world, many people associate the word "career" with a dull, lifeless office job that one works just to pay the bills. However, all careers should be about passion, excitement, and personal satisfaction—while also getting the bills paid, of course. So if you're a big fan of working with your hands, feeling the sun on your face, and enjoying the great outdoors, why would you pursue a job in an office setting? Here's the good news: you don't have to.

Imagine that you could get paid to sail the seas in search of fishing spots, guide people through national parks, or get your hands in the dirt and garden all day long. If that sounds appealing, you'll be happy to learn that there are countless opportunities in these fields—and others—for people who love nature. Unlike many career paths, a lot of these jobs are open to those who don't have a college degree, and sometimes they require little to no advanced training. In a lot of outdoors-related industries, hands-on experience and a strong work ethic are more important than a degree.

Just as in every field, you'll have to work your way up at a company or organization that offers nature-based work. You may start by working early or late, getting your hands dirty (often literally), and gaining valuable experience. However, if you can stick it out through the early phases, there's a lot of room to advance and start working as a manager, organizer, or administrator—most of the time accompanied by a nice pay raise.

If you'd rather stretch your legs than sit at a desk day in and day out, don't worry: there are workplaces for people like you all across the world. Whether you're growing Christmas trees, leading whale-watching expeditions, or protecting wildlands, there are plenty of cool outdoor careers out there.

CHAPTER 1

LITTLE GREEN IN THE BIG CITY

If you didn't grow up in a city, you're probably used to seeing and exploring the natural world. Large fields of green grass, towering trees of many varieties, and every color of wildflower imaginable are spread across the world's less metropolitan areas. But if you grew up in or near a city, you're probably not used to being able to appreciate the beauty of nature on a daily basis. In some urban areas, the only green to be seen is sprouting up from cracks

in the cement of an abandoned lot—certainly not a pleasant sight.

Enter the urban gardener, a person whose job it is to transform the concrete jungle. One of the most common methods of bringing nature to big cities is by starting and maintaining a community garden. At these locations, urban gardeners teach and encourage people from the local area to help them plant,

Urban gardeners add a splash of the natural world to cities all across the United States and Canada.

cultivate, and harvest all kinds of plants, from pretty flowers to nutritious vegetables. Growing food in some urban areas is a big deal, as members of the community may not have easy access to fresh produce without the help of an urban gardener. It's even possible for a community garden or another urban gardening project to expand into a small-scale farm, located right in the middle of the city and serving the needs of people well beyond the neighborhood.

URBAN GARDEN, URBAN RESPONSIBILITIES

An urban gardener works in—or helps operate and maintain—a community garden or urban farm. The need for talented, passionate urban gardeners is higher than ever, as the number of community gardens across the world is on the rise. According to the Trust for Public Land, there are nearly 30,000 community gardens across the United States' 100 largest cities.

The people involved in community gardening have the chance to combine a love of nature and knowledge of gardening and horticulture with a passion for helping others. Urban gardeners must be willing to pitch in and do some tough labor. Typical daily or weekly tasks include clearing and cleaning up vacant lots; maintaining equipment sheds, benches, and picnic tables; composting leaves and leftover produce; and, of course, weeding, planting,

STRIKING SUCCESS IN URBAN FARMING

Urban farming is spreading fast all across the United States and around the globe. Here are just a few success stories:

- In London, England, a 2009 program supported by then-mayor Boris Johnson saw nearly 100,000 London residents growing crops in more than 2,000 community gardens across the city.
- In 2010, 67 New York City urban gardens and farms participated in a study supported by the grassroots organization Farming Concrete. They grew 87,700 pounds (39,780 kg) of fresh produce—valued at nearly $200,000— in just 17 acres (6.8 ha).
- In 2011, 10 urban farms on 4.19 acres (1.7 ha) of land in Vancouver, British Columbia, sold $170,000 worth of produce. These farms also supported 30 paid employees.
- The Wood Street Farm Stand on Chicago's South Side is operated by the nonprofit organization Growing Home. This organization offers jobs to people who have barriers to traditional employment, such as criminal histories. Though the Wood Street Farm Stand is supported by only about .5 acre (.2 ha) of land, it has sold thousands of pounds of produce since its establishment.
- In New Orleans, a local organization called Grow Dat Youth Farm teaches young people to grow food in City Park. Children compete to see which group of kids can sell out first at local farmers markets, and they serve their produce at free breakfasts held in community buildings.

and harvesting in the gardens. If you learn the ropes by helping out with these basic tasks, you may be able to work your way up to assist with other activities in the garden.

In addition to growing delicious vegetables and beautiful flowers, many nonprofit "urban greening" or community gardening projects are devoted to providing environmental education for the people in the neighborhood. When working for one of these projects, you may be required to work in youth or after-school programs that promote nutrition and environmental awareness through the hands-on process of growing healthy foods.

Some gardeners help train volunteers who want to get involved. Others help sell the garden's produce at local farmers markets or to restaurants and local stores. Your experience working for a community garden could eventually lead to work in a variety of agricultural settings, such as a small farm, a private or public garden, a greenhouse, a tree nursery, or an outdoor classroom.

As you gain experience and get your hands dirty as an urban gardener, you may find yourself moving out of the weeds and into an administrative position within the organization. You may be able to start helping communities establish their own gardens, rather than setting them up with your own hands. In this position, you may be responsible for recruiting, instructing, and supporting volunteer leaders as they create and maintain productive community gardens. Other responsibilities might include:

- Providing advice on starting a neighbor-hood garden project
- Relaying accurate information on food growing and preservation
- Putting neighborhood gardeners in touch with local gardening resources
- Distributing donated seeds, plants, gardening supplies, and tools
- Seeking funding or sponsorship from sources both private (companies and individuals) and public (local, state, and/or federal governments)

While many people who lead community gardening organizations have advanced degrees in education, horticulture, or community development, extensive hands-on experience will allow you to pursue opportunities with these groups. Community college courses or certified training programs in education, community development, or horticulture/agriculture would be a plus if you want to really climb the ranks. You probably won't earn a lot of money in any of these jobs. The real reward of urban gardening is seeing a neighborhood transformed—both physically and socially—and getting to work with something you love every day.

The best way to become a gardener is to practice—and you can do that right in your own backyard.

GETTING YOUR TROWEL IN THE DIRT

How do you get started with urban gardening? The first step is simple: get out there and dig. Any relevant hands-on experience with gardening will help you pursue this career. Try volunteering with an existing community garden or urban farm in your area. Many of these establishments will offer internships or training programs for enthusiastic volunteers. Once you have your foot in the door, prove to your supervisors that you're a hard worker and good organizer. Keep your eye out for paying jobs. As you work your way up to higher job levels, you may find that you want to go back to school to study horticulture, education, or other subjects that will help you better serve your community. However, it's not necessary to have this advanced education to make a dependable, rewarding living as an urban gardener.

Many people will note that the most important part of a community garden is the community. Work on strengthening your people skills. Be able to communicate and cooperate with others. It takes many hands to run a successful community garden!

CHAPTER 2

THOSE WHO PROTECT
THE PARKS

If you enjoy nature, love the outdoors, and can't get enough of hiking, you're probably already deeply familiar with the job of a park ranger. A ranger's job is to patrol, maintain, and educate people about parks, both local and national. Perhaps the best-known employer of park rangers is the U.S. National Park Service (NPS), a large government body that supervises the country's more than 60 national parks. From the famous locations—like Yellowstone National Park, spread between Wyoming, Montana, and Idaho—to the hidden gems—like Cuyahoga Valley National Park, nestled in the heart of Ohio—working in the system of national parks across the United States is considered a dream opportunity for many young nature lovers.

Working as a national park ranger is tough, and getting a position can be even tougher. Even though the NPS employs about 28,000 people to protect and maintain the nation's parks, qualifying for a position is far from easy. It requires experience, training, and most of all, passion.

WHAT IT MEANS TO BE A RANGER

Because there are so many parks with so many different features and needs, it's difficult to generalize about the job of a park ranger. There are national parks spread all over the United States, and a ranger's duties are different at each one. For instance, a ranger posted at Glacier Bay National Park and Preserve in Alaska may have to deal with snow avalanches, while a ranger stationed in Death Valley National Park may have to search for and rescue dehydrated campers. The demands of varying climates and weather patterns require skilled hands to meet them.

A ranger's job is equal parts conservation and public relations. Park rangers are often expected to manage campgrounds, design and develop recreational activities and conservation programs, lead tours and nature walks for park visitors, and provide educational talks for children. They also work on conserving the natural world through habitat restoration and ecological projects. These include studying wildlife behavior and monitoring air and water quality in the park. Any given day might find rangers assisting stranded climbers, transporting injured park guests to hospitals, administering first aid, or enforcing the rules and regulations of the park. All of this is in addition to duties related to their long-term conservation goals.

BECOMING A RANGER

Experience—often supplemented with some form of on-the-job training—is the way to make it as a ranger. No formal college education is necessary to get started. Hands-on experience, on the other hand, is very valuable and will set you apart from other high school graduates.

To get started, you can volunteer or intern at a nature center, outdoor education center, or state or national park to get experience working outdoors and discover which duties and geographic areas you prefer. Try contacting a local forester, wildlife manager, or naturalist to inquire about such opportunities.

Many park rangers break into entry-level positions after high school, beginning their careers as

The national parks system of the United States is one of the best in the world; rangers with the NPS are responsible for protecting it.

seasonal rangers or as volunteers. Seasonal rangers may work in one park—which is fairly common—or travel from park to park, working at one in the winter, another in the summer. They usually perform the ranger equivalent of grunt work, taking care of tasks such as toll collecting, cleaning up campsites,

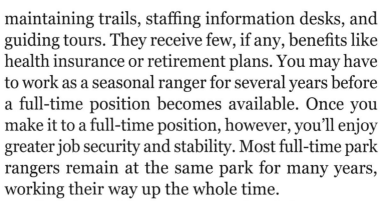

WORKING CLOSER TO HOME

The stereotypical image of a park ranger is someone who works in a remote forest or atop a mountain, isolated from society and working alone in the wilderness. You may be surprised to learn that park rangers can also work in urban and suburban areas. For instance, in New York City's Central Park, youth staff called discovery guides answer visitor questions. A visiting nature lover may discover a plant they can't identify—that's where a discovery guide comes in. As an expert in the local plants and ecosystem, they'll be able to tell the park visitor its species and probably even some fun facts.

This is just one example of an urban park ranger job—many cities and towns in the United States feature lush natural attractions, and many of them require maintenance and conservation professionals to work the grounds. Look for more information about these potential opportunities by visiting your local parks' websites.

maintaining trails, staffing information desks, and guiding tours. They receive few, if any, benefits like health insurance or retirement plans. You may have to work as a seasonal ranger for several years before a full-time position becomes available. Once you make it to a full-time position, however, you'll enjoy greater job security and stability. Most full-time park rangers remain at the same park for many years, working their way up the whole time.

The orientation programs and training a ranger receives on the job is sometimes supplemented with formal training courses offered by the NPS. It's also a good idea to take courses on your own in environmental science, park management, natural history, forestry, outdoor recreation, and/or communications during seasonal breaks. If you take the time to be formally educated, you can combine that knowledge with real-world experience—which will improve your chances of landing a full-time ranger position. Some park ranger positions do require a bachelor's degree, while a master's degree is helpful for those hoping to become supervisors and managers.

NATURAL NATIONAL TREASURES

Some of the United States' most incredible outdoor experiences can be discovered within the national parks system. Here are a few once-in-a-lifetime experiences that park rangers help preserve for the public:

- **Rafting the Grand Canyon.** A visit to the Grand Canyon is a must for any outdoors lover. The incredible sight of the massive natural chasm is both humbling and awe-inspiring. A few lucky visitors to the park—chosen by a lottery—are permitted to raft down the river at the canyon's base.
- **Viewing the aurora borealis.** Have you ever longed to see the aurora borealis, or northern lights? Most common near the North Pole, this unique natural

phenomenon occurs when solar wind reaches Earth's atmosphere, creating a spectacular show of colored lights in the sky. At Alaska's Denali National Park, the northern lights are such a popular attrac-

Because the United States contains so many different geographic areas, its parks offer a wide variety of amazing sights, such as the aurora borealis.

tion that local hotels offer to wake sleeping guests when the lights appear.

- **Climbing a volcano.** The main attraction at Hawai'i Volcanoes National Park is the two active volcanoes. Visitors can walk around a volcano's edge and maybe  catch a glimpse of the magma that burns deep within Earth's surface. The lava flows at the park reach temperatures of 2,100 degrees Fahrenheit (1,149 degrees Celsius)!
- **Bat-watching in Carlsbad Caverns National Park.** During the summer and fall, Carlsbad Caverns in New Mexico is home to a colony of 400,000 Mexican free-tailed bats. You can watch the nocturnal bats emerge in the evening as a massive group, eager to hunt insects. They return in the morning to sleep the day away in the dark of the caverns.
- **Canoeing in Everglades National Park.** Canoe or kayak serene

waterways in the Everglades, a park in Florida that features peaceful, exotic swamps and islands made of mangrove trees. Along the way, you might glimpse dolphins, manatees, and crocodiles, among other wildlife.

- **Sandboarding in Great Sand Dunes National Park and Preserve.** You'll find these stunning sand dunes in an unexpected location: the middle of landlocked Colorado. Thrill seekers bring snowboards and "sandboard" down the fluffy white dunes. It's like skiing, but without the winter gear!

LOOK AROUND FOR IT

Most park rangers will advise aspiring rangers to be open-minded with respect to moving around. After all, national parks jobs don't open up all that frequently. Opportunities are more abundant in urban areas—but with a little experience, you'll have a greater ability to pick the region in which you would most like to work. Experience gained from seasonal work is directly applicable to your pursuit for a permanent position.

Full-time rangers will often receive a complete government benefits package, which includes overtime pay, paid vacations, holiday time, sick leave, health insurance, and retirement benefits. In some cases, rangers live in government-provided housing within the park. Most rangers feel that this generous benefits package offsets their relatively low pay. As another plus, rangers are passionate about their work, making these positions both desirable and satisfying.

CHAPTER 3

HARVESTING THE SEAS

Many people who fish do it for fun. They like to go out on a boat, relax in the sun, and hook a few big ones. Commercial fishing, however, isn't relaxing at all. Working on a fishing boat is physically demanding, mentally difficult, and sometimes dangerous. A lot of commercial fishing vessels must travel to isolated locations in search of the best hauls, which means a lot of time away from home and a lot of time out in bad weather.

Though there are a lot of potentially negative aspects of a career as a fisher, the job offers a lot of positives as well. For instance, living for weeks or months at a time on the open water can be enjoyable, and deckhands are often given a lot of independence on the boat once they've proven themselves. On top of that, many commercial fishers are nature lovers, and they get a chance to spend time among some of the greatest natural landscapes in the world.

THE BASICS OF LARGE-SCALE FISHING

Commercial fishers—as their title implies—catch fish and other marine life, such as lobsters and shrimp, to be sold as food, bait, or animal feed. They often fish hundreds of miles from shore in large boats that can hold tens of thousands of pounds of fish. They may spend weeks or months at a time sailing, only returning to their home port to offload fish and rest before the next trip. Work on a commercial fishing ship is a repeated cycle of difficult activity followed by quiet lulls. Netting and hauling in the fish are both exhausting tasks that require great physical strength and endurance. Though there is some downtime on the ship, most commercial fishers are only able to enjoy long periods of rest when the ship is in its home port or on the way to another fishing ground.

Traveling between fishing grounds is important, as commercial fishers must go to wherever the fish are. Seasonal as well as year-round jobs are available in parts of Canada, Alaska, New England, Ireland, Mexico, Florida, and Seattle—wherever there is port access to freshwater or saltwater fish and it's permissible to catch and sell marine animals.

Most commercial fishing vessels are staffed with a crew that includes several officers: a captain, a first

Commercial fishers bring popular seafood products from the water to tables all over the world.

mate, and a boatswain. At the bottom of the totem pole are the deckhands. Deckhands are responsible for loading and unloading supplies and equipment; untying the lines that moor the ship to the dock; letting out and hauling in the nets; cleaning, preserving, and storing the catch; and unloading the catch upon

return to port. They're also responsible for keeping the decks clear and clean, and they sometimes play a part in maintaining the ship's engines and equipment so the vessel continues running smoothly. Deckhands must be in good health, extremely coordinated and mechanically inclined, and very strong. Most commercial fishers begin their careers as deckhands.

The boatswain acts as a supervisor for the deckhands, directing them in the performance of the ship's sailing and fishing operations. The boatswain also repairs fishing gear, equipment, and nets. The first mate serves as the captain's direct assistant and is capable of operating the ship and directing the crew when the captain is off duty. The first mate also organizes and oversees the actual fishing activity and sailing operations, such as gathering, preserving, storing, and unloading the catch and maintaining or repairing the ship. They must be able to perform all of the captain's duties as well as those of the deckhands

FAST FISHING FACTS

Commercial fishing is a challenging profession, but those who love it wouldn't choose any other life. Here are a few interesting facts about commercial fishing:

- According to the U.S. National Oceanic and Atmospheric Administration (NOAA), the United States exported 1,554,023 tons (1,408,879 mt) of edible fishery products in 2017, valued at $5.4 billion.
- Commercial fishing has one of the highest rates of self-employed workers in the North American workforce.
- With modern technology and amenities, fishing boats are much more comfortable today than they used to be. Many now include televisions and shower stalls.
- Around 75 percent of all U.S. commercial fishing contributes to the production of human-grade food products, including frozen seafood meals.

and the boatswain, should an emergency make their assistance necessary.

The most powerful person on a ship, a captain plans and supervises the entire fishing expedition. Before each trip out to sea, the captain must draw up an operating budget; decide what type of fish will be pursued; figure out where the crew will fish and how the fish will be caught; map out how long the trip will last; and organize buyers for the catch following their return to port. The captain also makes sure the vessel is in proper working order, buys the necessary supplies and equipment, keeps track of weather information, and charts the ship's course using compasses, charts, and tables. A captain must have a thorough knowledge of navigation, boat handling, weather patterns, communication techniques, and use of electronic gear. They must also be able to make good decisions quickly and calmly in emergencies, train and manage a crew with skill and tact, and ensure that fish are handled properly so that consumers can safely eat them. Another important component of a captain's responsibilities is making sure that all fishing is done within the legal limits and through the legal methods. Almost all captains are self-employed, and many own at least some share of their ship.

SETTING OUT TO SEA

The most common way to get a job on a fishing vessel is to walk the docks at the closest fishing port, going from boat to boat asking captains if they have work available. Some would-be fishers find work in fish processing plants in fishing towns while they wait to find an opportunity as a deckhand.

No formal academic requirements exist for most fishing work. Many fishers learn the trade from family members already working in the industry. In addition, some community colleges and universities offer courses in seamanship, boat operations, marine safety, navigation, boat repair and maintenance, and

Though it's not an outdoors-based job, working in fish processing can help you land a job on a fishing vessel.

first aid. In some places, you may need a crewman's license before you can get hired. Research the local regulations in the area in which you plan to work. If you're lucky enough to be hired onto a boat, you'll want to find out about the reputation of your boat's company and captain. Some boats might be unsafe, and others might be known to cheat deckhands. You are your own greatest advocate, so make sure you're only working in a safe, reputable environment.

A WAVY WORKPLACE

According to the Bureau of Labor Statistics, there are nearly 40,000 fishers and fishing boat operators nationwide. Though this number seems very large, the industry is actually projected to shrink over time. Between 2018 and 2028, the BLS predicts a 2 percent decrease in available jobs. Fishing is a hard business, mainly because pollution and excessive fishing have depleted fish stocks. The number of permits issued to fishers has declined in an attempt to allow fish populations to rebound. Because the industry is not able to naturally grow, it's becoming more difficult to break into the field.

Earnings for the average fisher tend to be highest in the summer and autumn and lowest during the winter. Many fishers work full-time on a vessel for only part of the year, taking other jobs during the off-season to earn more money. Many of them work in fish processing plants, in stores that sell fishing and boating equipment, and in construction. However, it's possible to work on a fishing boat full-time, so long as you can accept slightly lower pay during slower months.

CHAPTER 4

GIVE US A (RANCH) HAND

For many, the images of cowboys and ranches are located firmly in the past. In many rural areas of the United States, however, working on a real ranch is still an everyday way of life. Livestock must be tended, and it's up to passionate, dedicated ranch hands to take care of these animals. In addition to raising farm animals, some ranches (called dude ranches) are open to tourists and offer educational programs to guests. Often, ranch hands at a dude ranch are expected to put on a smile and lead these seminars and hands-on experiences. This requires good communication and people skills—in addition to the talents required for taking care of livestock when it's time to demonstrate the work.

Ranch hands must know a lot about animal care and how to work with their hands—and they must love working outside.

HELPING HANDS

The most basic duties of a ranch hand—sometimes called a wrangler—on a working ranch are tending livestock and repairing and cleaning fences, ranch buildings, and equipment. Taking care of livestock usually includes feeding, birthing, branding, shearing, roping, sorting, pasturing, herding, and grooming the various animals on the ranch. It also involves caring for the health of the horses, cattle, poultry, pigs, and sometimes sheep. After raising healthy animals

through this attentive care, ranch hands will also be responsible for hauling the livestock to market or to a shipping terminal.

Horses are particularly important to the operation of a successful ranch, whether it's a working or dude ranch. As such, tending to horses is one of the most crucial tasks that a wrangler must attend to. At a working ranch, horses are used to herd cattle. At

Dude ranches are popular tourist attractions, and ranch hands at these establishments must be able to connect with guests.

a dude ranch, the horses are typically younger and used for taking guests on horseback rides around the compound. The animals' health and well-being are very important. Horse-related duties include daily brushing and grooming, tack and equipment upkeep and repair, and providing basic veterinary care.

In addition to taking excellent care of the working animals, ranch hands must be able to construct and mend fences, maintain trails around the property, and clean out the corrals.

On dude ranches, wranglers require not only considerable skill in horsemanship and stable operation, but also good interpersonal skills. Ranch hands at these locations must be able to interact with both adult guests and their children, all of whom are there for a positive and educational experience. A good ranch hand may take guests on overnight hiking and fishing trips or cattle drives, teach basic riding skills, lead horseback riding and river rafting expeditions, and perhaps get behind the wheel for some off-road adventures. These positions on dude ranches generally involve lots of hard work, long hours (generally dawn to dusk), and participation in guest activities in the evening, such as line dances, cookouts, hayrides, and staff talent shows. Work at these ranches is seasonal. While pay tends to be low, the compensation package will often include room and board, a share of the overall tips, and the use of the facilities and horses when off duty. A job at a dude ranch is also a great tool for gaining valuable experience working with various species of livestock, which can be used to advance in the industry or explore other positions outside it.

DUDE, WHERE'S MY RANCH?

In the late 1800s, following the U.S. Civil War, cattle ranching became a booming business in the West. A man named Howard Eaton and his two brothers moved west to the Dakotas, where they founded a cattle ranch. They wrote letters to friends back east, describing their adventures and the natural beauty of the land around them. One of those letters was published in a New York newspaper, where it attracted the attention of none other than Teddy Roosevelt. Roosevelt was so intrigued by the Eatons' adventures that he purchased a ranch near theirs, which he often visited to go hunting and riding. Suddenly, the Eatons found that—like Roosevelt—many of their eastern friends wanted to visit. They welcomed hundreds of visitors—until they realized how much the guests were costing them. Not wanting to put the Eatons in a financially stressful situation, the guests (or "dudes") started to pay for their room and board voluntarily. Just like that, an American tradition was created: the dude ranch, at which visitors can ride, perform ranch chores, and socialize with the ranch owners and staff.

As time marched on and the cattle business became less stable, more ranchers in Montana, Wyoming, and other Western states began to open up their homes to guests as dude ranches. Today, there are dude ranches all over the United States and Canada, each of which offers its own unique take on the ranch experience for vacationers.

WORKING YOUR WAY IN

You don't need a formal education to succeed in this line of work: on-the-job training and experience are the best schooling. Fortunately, seasonal work as a ranch hand is not generally hard to find. Other ranch jobs to consider as a starting point include children's counselor, groomer, cook, maid, waitstaff member, maintenance worker, or—in the winter months— cross-country ski instructor. Besides previous work experience, CPR and first-aid certification are helpful credentials. Though the animals working at dude ranches are well trained and generally peaceful, it's always possible that someone could get kicked by a horse or rammed by a sheep. In these emergency situations, a wrangler with basic emergency medical qualifications will be highly valuable.

If you hope to advance to a position as a ranch foreman—or even own your own ranch someday— you should consider a community college or university degree in agricultural production, agricultural economics, animal husbandry, or veterinary medicine. It's easy to get in on the ground level in this industry with only a high school education, but moving upward can require more advanced classroom training.

MODERNIZING THE RANCH

Dude ranches are popular destinations for families who want a unique vacation, so there are growing opportunities in this field. You have many geographic options if you're interested in pursuing employment as a ranch hand. The most widespread jobs will be in Arizona, California, Colorado, Montana, Nevada, New Mexico, New York, Texas, Washington, or Wyoming. Ranches can also be found in parts of Hawaii, Mexico, Argentina, Brazil, Alberta, and British Columbia, as well as many other places around the world. The only limit to your employment opportunities is your imagination and your willingness to travel.

CHAPTER 5

WORKING THE RIVERS

Water has always been a human necessity, but it can also be a source of fun. If you're brave enough to pit yourself, your boat, and your oar against raging rapids on a winding river, you may want to consider a job as a river guide. As an employee of a river rafting company, you can take on the responsibility of leading groups of inexperienced amateurs or seasoned rafters, finding fun currents for the group to enjoy.

Even if the high-stakes world of white-water rafting is not your speed, working on a river leading other kinds of tours can be highly rewarding and mentally satisfying. People travel far and wide to spend time on the world's vast network of rivers, and there is an entire industry dedicated to connecting tourists to information and experiences along local rivers.

TAMING RAGING WATERS

Picture it: bright sun overhead, it's you versus a wild river. With twists and turns and unpredictable rapids, the only things keeping you from capsizing are your skill and experience. A seasoned river guide knows how to read the water and spot its hidden dangers. River guides are experts in all areas of outdoorsmanship, emergency survival, and the safe management of a small craft on swift water. Guides must teach their team the basics of safety and rafting techniques and be prepared for unexpected emergencies on the river. Quick decisions must be made, and the guide is the person who must make them.

The most common way to learn how to be a river guide is to attend a school or training program specifically for people who want to become guides. Specially designed training sessions—which take several days to a week to complete—are run by many different companies (usually outdoors outfitters) and typically have an entrance fee. Though the idea of paying to get trained in this profession may be off-putting, many tour companies expect all their employees to have a baseline of important knowledge before applying. If you have a certificate from a reputable training school, your potential employer will have to do less on-the-job training, meaning you can get out on the water quicker. While you may

Rivers around the world are a source of food, water, and, of course, entertaining adventures.

find a company that's willing to hire you as a river guide without formal training, your lack of experience will likely lead to lower starting pay. Spending a little money up front to get certified on your own will help you earn a better wage. In addition, an outfitter who hires inexperienced guides may not be reputable and could endanger staff and customers

with shoddy equipment and negligent practices.

The best path to landing a good guide job is to sign up for a rafting course. Gaining this experience will get you prepared to be a desirable applicant for an open position at a respected touring company. Working an entry-level job, in turn, may allow you to start your own river tour company in the future. The school you choose should have experienced, knowledgeable teachers and mentors on its staff. Every aspect of guiding a raft downriver should be taught. Skills include everything from "reading" white water (predicting its flow and strength based on its surface appearance), maneuvering boats, tying knots, safely preparing food, composting, and recycling. A workshop on white-water emergency and rescue techniques should be included in any quality course. Generally, students supply some of their own gear—such as a tent, sleeping bag, sleeping pad, wet and dry suits, river shoes, and outdoor clothing—for these training sessions. This can help reduce the overall cost to you.

A good river school should maintain a low instructor-to-student ratio (such as one teacher for every four or five students) in order to ensure that each student is given proper individual attention and firsthand practice. In addition to instruction, students should be asked to participate in carefully supervised solo river sessions, in which they will have the chance to put theory into practice. You should use this time to discover solutions to difficulties on your own, which will raise your confidence—you'll need to be confident and comfortable if you want to lead your own expeditions. Some schools recommend that students take courses in first aid and CPR, such as with the American Red Cross, and read about river rafting before enrolling in a training program. It's also a good idea to spend some time playing around in an oar boat on a lake. Try practicing by sitting, holding the oars, and being comfortable in the boat before taking on any tough rivers or rapids.

A RIVER OF RESPONSIBILITIES

As a river guide, you'll have to observe certain safety codes and practices whenever you take a vessel out for white-water rafting. Here are some common safety tips for river guides:

- Make sure that everyone in your party is a competent swimmer.

- Be sure that everyone is wearing a life preserver, appropriate shoulder protection, and a correctly fitted helmet.
- Don't enter a rapid unless you are reasonably sure that you can get through it without injury or risk.
- Make sure that each boat contains at least three people and a party contains no fewer than two boats. Never boat alone.
- Have a realistic sense of your skills and the ability of your guests, taking into account their fitness, age, anxiety levels, and health. Don't attempt to navigate rapids that are beyond your party's abilities.
- Be well trained in rescue and self-rescue skills, CPR, and first aid. Carry the equipment necessary for unexpected emergencies, such as bandages, whistles, flashlights, folding saws, guidebooks, maps, food, waterproof matches, extra clothing, and repair kits.
- Check that your boat and gear are all in good working order well before the expedition. Test any new equipment before you take a party downriver.
- Never lead a party while you or the guests are under the influence of drugs and alcohol, and don't allow members of your party to partake in either during the expedition. Drugs and alcohol dull reflexes and impair decision-making ability.

A river guide's job is—first and foremost—to navigate guests down a river safely and enjoyably. Often, guides are also expected to prepare food for the trip, load and unload the vehicle bringing guests to the river, and provide information on the natural flora, fauna, and geology of the area. In some states, guides

Though working as a river guide can be fun, it's important to keep everyone's safety in the front of your mind.

must be officially licensed before they're allowed to lead trips on their own.

River guide work is often seasonal since some rivers dry up in the summer—and nobody wants to slowly drift down a partially frozen river in the snow! However, it's possible to work as a river guide in many different countries around the world, traveling year-round to wherever the job opportunities lie.

SPORTING OUTDOORS

If you're athletically talented and enjoy working with people, but white-water rafting doesn't appeal to you, there are a lot of other jobs that will allow you to make a living by teaching exciting out-door sports. Here are some other careers that you might consider:

•Rock climbing instructor
•Skiing or snowboarding instructor
•Waterskiing instructor
•Surfing instructor
•Scuba diving instructor
•Snorkeling guide or instructor
•Sailing instructor
•Horseback riding guide or instructor
•Mountain biking instructor

Of course, becoming an expert in these sports is not without cost, both physical and financial. You'll have to invest time and money at the outset as you prepare yourself to become a professional—and lessons in these sports can be expensive. In addition, you'll have to possess some level of talent with any activity you want to teach—otherwise, people wouldn't be willing to pay for your services. However, if you discover a passion for one of these activities, you may find yourself on the road to an exciting new job!

CHAPTER 6

WHALE-WATCHING WORK

Though the age of great ocean explorers may be past, there is still excitement and professional satisfaction to be found aboard a ship sailing the seas—even if that ship is close to home. In many port towns across the United States and around the globe, whale-watching expeditions set out every single day, led by naturalists who want to bring guests closer to some of the world's most incredible animals. In addition to good people skills and a passion for whales, a great whale-watching guide must be comfortable on a boat and able to lead guests and other crew members in the event of an emergency.

FINDING GENTLE GIANTS

Humans have long been fascinated by marine life, but commercial whale watching didn't start appearing until around 1955 in North America along the southern California coast. Whale watching as an

Thousands of people hit the high seas every year to catch a glimpse of whales.

industry today is booming. Tours sail the oceans and bays of more than 80 countries in search of the ocean's largest inhabitants. Supported by tourists and locals alike, the whale tourism industry, as it's sometimes called, sees yearly revenues in excess of $2 billion. Millions of conservation enthusiasts

all around the world set out to sea every year to see all kinds of majestic marine animals.

Whale and Dolphin Conservation (WDC), a charity that supports worldwide marine conservation efforts, specifies that a safe whale-watching boat includes an experienced skipper (or captain) and crew who are well trained in first aid and rescue skills. Members of the crew aren't just working the ship—they're responsible for educating the passengers about the whales and other marine life observed during an outing. Many whale-watching operations invite research scientists on board, and crew members may assist in their research projects.

According to WDC, good guides must be able to demonstrate several valuable characteristics. They should be lively and entertaining for passengers and knowledgeable about the local marine life. They must be able to interpret the behavior of whales spotted on

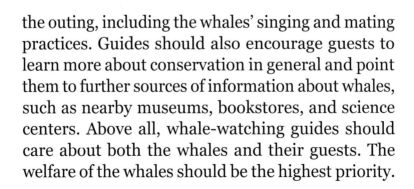

WHAT TO KNOW ABOUT WHALES

Whales are among the planet's most fascinating creatures. Here are just a few of the many incredible facts about whales:

- There are 90 different living species of whales.
- A group of large whales is called a pod.
- Each winter, California gray whales travel down the Pacific Coast from their summer feeding grounds (in the Bering Sea and Arctic Ocean) to Mexico's Baja Peninsula, where they breed and give birth. It's the longest mammal migration on Earth at around 12,000 miles (19,312 km) round trip each year.
- Male humpback whales "sing" to each other. They generate long, low tones that echo through the water. They also attract mates by breaching (rising above the water's surface) or slapping their tails down on the waves.
- Whales are marine mammals, not fish. Like all mammals, they feed their offspring with milk.
- Evolutionary scientists believe that the ancient ancestors of whales walked on land on four legs.

the outing, including the whales' singing and mating practices. Guides should also encourage guests to learn more about conservation in general and point them to further sources of information about whales, such as nearby museums, bookstores, and science centers. Above all, whale-watching guides should care about both the whales and their guests. The welfare of the whales should be the highest priority.

Whales come in many different shapes and sizes, and they're all capable of capturing the imagination.

A whale should never be disturbed or endangered to give guests a closer view or bigger thrill. Nor should the lives of passengers be threatened by reckless behavior.

A DIFFERENT KIND OF WHALING

Today, commercial whale watching is a worldwide phenomenon, with tourist numbers in the millions and revenues in the billions. However, whale watching as an industry has humble origins. In 1955, a San Diego fisherman—Chuck Chamberlin—put together the first modern-style whale-watching expedition. For just $1, tourists could ride on his boat and search the waters of southern California for gray whales. The idea began to spread to other fishermen, who began taking customers out to sea. Whale expert Raymond Gilmore joined the movement as well when he began offering trips led by naturalists. Soon, many people were traveling to the West Coast just to embark on a whale-watching adventure.

By the 1970s, whale-watching tours had also appeared on the East Coast, and in 1980, a Spanish fisherman began offering similar expeditions in Gibraltar Bay. Before long, whale-watching tours were also being offered in the Caribbean, South America, Australia, New Zealand, and Japan. What began as one fisherman's attempt to make a little extra money in the offseason became a huge global industry.

WORK YOUR WAY IN

Because the whale-watching industry is so prosperous, there are many large corporations in the space. These companies often offer internships to interested youth. For instance, the Blue Ocean Society for Marine Conservation offers internships with a focus on education. Interns are able to go out on boats with passengers, teach classes, and answer questions about whales. The Whale Center of New England offers summer internships in which interns educate the public on whale-watching boats and work the counter at a visitor center. Internships with established touring companies can be a great way to get your foot in the door, learn about the whale-watching business, and gain valuable experience.

DAILY DUTIES IN WHALE WATCHING

Whale-watching professionals need to be personable, friendly, and tough. A working knowledge of basic boating and water safety skills is helpful. A strong interest in whale biology and behavior is a must. It's also vital to have good customer service skills and the ability to calmly and quickly deal with problems and emergencies. The types of problems that could emerge on a whale-watching boat include frightened children, seasick passengers, and sudden storms.

Be sure to choose a reputable operator that won't take advantage of you, harm or endanger the whales, or put the safety of the guests at risk. You won't get rich as a whale-watching guide. You'll most likely draw a modest salary or hourly wage—but some operators encourage tipping, which can be a nice incentive to keep up your positive attitude.

CHAPTER 7

GREEN THUMB GROUNDSKEEPING

A dream job for a nature lover may have some of these characteristics: spending a lot of time outside; working with plants (and sometimes animals); and being able to get your hands dirty. One job that can meet all these wishes—while adding other perks as well—is that of a groundskeeper. People have long made careers arranging, implementing, and maintaining natural beauty for businesses, governments, and private clients. More impressively, many have done this without an advanced degree—and you can, too, if you're willing to take on physically tough work.

HOW DO YOU "KEEP" GROUND?

Groundskeepers—also called landscapers—are responsible for the design and maintenance of healthy lawns and gardens. They maintain the grounds of industrial, commercial, or public property, such as parks and botanical gardens. They may also maintain a variety of specific facilities, including athletic fields, golf courses, and cemeteries. On top of that, some groundskeepers are also tasked with maintaining indoor greenery, such as the lush displays often found in malls, hotels, and interior exhibits in botanical gardens.

Landscapers perform many facets of grounds work, such as mowing, raking, trimming, landscaping, laying sod, watering, fertilizing, digging, and gardening. To help them complete these tasks, they use hand tools, such as shovels, rakes, pruning shears, saws, and hedge clippers. They also operate a variety of power equipment, including riding mowers, snowblowers, chain saws, loaders, tractors, and field marking equipment. That's a lot to keep track of!

Many landscaping and groundskeeping jobs are seasonal. Demand for grounds work is highest during the spring, summer, and fall months, when temperatures are pleasant and growth is thriving. Most of a

Healthy green grass and shrubs are almost always the result of good care—often by a professional groundskeeper.

groundskeeper's work is performed outdoors. The digging of holes, lifting of young trees, and operation of heavy machinery requires a lot of strength and stamina. Additionally, because most groundskeeping work is done during warmer months, you must be able to withstand the heat—sunscreen and proper attire are must-haves in this industry.

Most entry-level jobs in the field require no college education. In fact, some new hires in landscaping jobs may not even have a high school diploma. Instead, training in landscaping techniques and the operation of mowers, trimmers, leaf blowers, and tractors occurs on the job as needed. Starting wages tend to be quite low, but for nature lovers, the smaller paycheck is offset by the time spent outside and the satisfaction of participating in the beautification of their surroundings. Additionally, there's a lot of job security in the field—there will always be a need for someone with a green thumb and a good attitude toward maintaining grounds. The Bureau of Labor Statistics estimates that growth in the field will be far above average, rising 9 percent between 2018 and 2028.

There are a number of other careers that share characteristics with groundskeeping. Nursery and greenhouse workers, for instance, grow the plants, flowers, shrubs, and trees that will eventually be planted by landscapers. Landscape contractors make the designs of landscape architects into reality. They are tasked with planting trees, shrubs, and flowers; laying sod; and the placement of benches, statues, and other important design elements. They may also install lighting and sprinkler systems in a natural area and build footpaths, patios, decks, and fountains. The landscape contractor generally directs a supervisor, who in turn oversees the landscape laborers who actually perform all the grounds work.

Groundskeeping laborers tend to focus on the maintenance of specialized facilities, such as playing fields, golf courses, parks, college campuses, and cemeteries. Their duties are often identical to those of landscape laborers but may also include clearing snow from walkways and parking lots; maintaining and replacing sidewalks, planters, fountains, pools, fences, and benches; and doing turf care and painting.

EMPLOYMENT OPPORTUNITIES

All landowning entities—including large corporations, amusement parks, professional sports organizations, the government, schools and universities, homeowners, apartment complexes, and city parks— have a need for natural beautification and upkeep of their grounds. Demand has consistently increased for landscaping and groundskeeping services as the construction of commercial and residential complexes, homes, parks, and highways has grown. In addition, turnover among landscapers and groundskeepers is high, so it's typically easy to find an entry-level job. This means groundskeepers can find satisfying work in just about any location: urban, rural, or suburban. You can work as part of the groundskeeping staff at a large institution, for a private contractor, or even go into business for yourself.

SPORTS: MORE THAN ATHLETICS

One major segment of the groundskeeping industry is tending to the very particular needs of athletic fields—especially those used by professional athletes. These include the fields and courts on which football, baseball, golf, and tennis are played. The grass or turf on these playing surfaces must be perfectly maintained and properly drained through the use of tractors, aerators, fertilizers, and insecticides. Even artificial turf must be vacuumed, repaired, and disinfected between uses. Workers who care for athletic fields keep natural and artificial turf fields in top condition, mark out boundaries, and paint the fields with team logos and names before events. Workers who maintain golf courses are called greenkeepers. They do many of the same things that other groundskeepers do but also relocate the holes on putting greens and repair and paint ball washers, benches, and tee markers. Imagine the satisfaction of seeing your handiwork on television while your favorite team plays on the field that you tended with your own two hands!

GETTING IN ON THE GROUND FLOOR

Because nearly all groundskeepers learn through on-the-job training, you can get started in the business with little more than a high school diploma—or an equivalent—and a driver's license. You should be able to demonstrate literacy and good interpersonal skills. The best education for an aspiring landscape professional is the one obtained by watching more

Golf courses require a huge amount of maintenance. Golfers will know when the greens haven't been properly taken care of.

experienced workers on the job—and getting your own hands dirty doesn't hurt. You will learn skills like planting, cultivating, pruning trees, and fertilizing lawns, trees, and shrubs. Inexpensive courses in gardening and horticulture are often available at nurseries and greenhouses; these can provide a solid background for your career. Building up a knowledge base by attending classes can also be a way for you to advance in the field.

CHAPTER 8

HOW LOVELY ARE YOUR BRANCHES

There are few holidays as widely loved as Christmas, and business during the holiday season—both in the United States and across the world—is explosive. This is especially true for any business that sells traditional Christmas items, like evergreen trees. Though Christmas is only one day a year, and most people have a tree for only a few weeks during the season, Christmas tree farmers are hard at work every month of the year. They get to spend time outdoors, planting and cultivating their products, preparing them for the booming holidays that come every year. If you love planting and growing, this may be the job for you—especially if you may want to one day own your own business, as many Christmas tree farmers do.

MORE THAN PINE NEEDLES

Before Christianity spread across Europe, evergreen plants were an important part of the midwinter celebrations held by pagan Europeans. Ancient Europeans believed that decorating with evergreen boughs brought good luck and helped keep evil spirits away from a home or village. This practice was especially associated with a day that held special significance for pagans: the shortest day of the year, called the winter solstice. Over time, many traditional solstice practices became Christmas traditions.

The modern Christmas tree tradition originated in Germany. Across the country, families began to place Christmas trees inside their homes around the 16th century. Some believe that influential church reformer Martin Luther was the first to add candles to the Christmas tree. According to legend, he was attempting to capture the beauty of stars glimpsed through dark evergreen boughs in the winter season. German immigrants brought the Christmas tree tradition to America, but the practice did not immediately catch on beyond the German American community.

It took a celebrity couple to make the Christmas tree fashionable. In 1840, Britain's popular young Queen Victoria married Prince Albert, her German cousin. The young couple captured the public's interest and imagination. In 1846, the *London News* published an illustration of the royal family and their children decorating a Christmas tree

The practice of celebrating in winter with an evergreen tree has deep historical roots.

together. Soon, fashionable British families began to imitate the royals by setting up their own Christmas trees, complete with festive decorations. The tradition quickly became popular with Americans who wanted to keep up with the trend. Today, it's nearly impossible to imagine the Christmas season without Christmas trees!

EVERGREEN GARDENING?

The up-front investment required to start a tree farm can be intimidating, especially because it takes six to twelve years for the first crop of evergreens to grow to selling size. One of the reasons Christmas tree farming can be profitable, however, is that pine trees can flourish on marginal—or less fertile—land. This type of land is far less expensive to purchase than rich farmland, which is commonly used for growing consumable crops.

Christmas tree farmers need to be knowledgeable about trees in general and about popular Christmas tree varieties in particular. A single crop of trees requires a full year's work, and the yield isn't always high. Approximately 2,000 trees can be planted per acre (0.4 ha) on the average tree farm, but only 750 to 1,500 trees will survive to harvest. The good news is that around 30 million trees are sold each year, resulting in annual sales of between $360 and $540 million—that's big business.

A typical Christmas tree farm's cycle begins in March and April, when farmers plant the year's crop

TREE TRIVIA

The National Christmas Tree Association (NCTA) is a professional organization that represents hundreds of farms and farmers who grow trees for a living. The group works to educate people about the industry and has reported these facts about Christmas tree production in the United States:

- U.S. consumers purchase around 25 to 30 million Christmas trees each year.
- For every Christmas tree harvested, two or three seedlings are planted in its place for the next growing season.
- There are about 15,000 Christmas tree farmers in North America, and more than 100,000 people are employed full-time or part-time in the industry.
- There are around 350 million Christmas trees growing in U.S. soil.
- Christmas trees are grown across all 50 U.S. states.
- The average growing time for a Christmas tree is seven years.

with seedlings that are grown in beds or greenhouses. A seedling is a small tree that is usually 8 to 16 inches (20.3 to 40.6 cm) tall. The planting is done either by hand or with the help of a planting machine that is mounted on a tractor. If it's done by hand, this is typically work reserved for entry-level employees.

In the spring and summer, farmers must pay close attention to the upkeep of the grounds where their trees grow. Weeds and overgrown grass—which compete with the trees for both space and water—can damage the undersides of the trees, making them less attractive and harder to sell. Properly maintaining the farmland also helps prevent potential fires, as dry or overgrown grasses and weeds can be hazardous. The grass between the trees must be mowed, and many farmers manage weeds by covering them with piles of mulch. Eliminating grass and weeds will also keep away mice, which often kill young trees by eating the bark.

Insects and disease can become a problem during the evergreen offseason. Pruning or removal of infested and diseased trees can help control the problem and prevent it from spreading to other trees in the crop. Though it's difficult to willingly throw out trees that could potentially make money, failure to do so could result in widespread trouble down the road—and the loss of even more money.

During the summer months, the baby trees are shaped through pruning. This helps produce the cone shape and dense foliage growth that customers look for in a Christmas tree. Pruning prevents the trees from growing too tall and encourages them to branch more quickly, creating a thick, bushy appearance. Without attentive care at the earliest stages of a tree's life, it won't grow to become a desirable Christmas tree.

Fall represents the busiest time of year for Christmas tree farmers. By October, the trees are ready to be harvested and shipped. Some farmers allow

The weeks and months before Christmas are the best times for a tree farmer, as their products will be in high demand.

families to visit the farm, where they'll walk the fields and choose and cut their own trees. Other farmers harvest the trees themselves and gather the cut trees together, selling them in an open area near the farm's entrance. Still others harvest the trees and ship them to city vendors. Before a tree is shipped, it

must be shaken out and baled. In this process, a machine presses the tree's branches against the trunk and secures them in place with twine or plastic netting. This protects the tree from damage to the branches and makes it easier to handle when loading and unloading. However farmers choose to harvest and sell them, the trees must be ready for the buyers, who can show up as early as the end of November.

For a short while before and after Christmas Day, tree farmers can take some time off and rest after a year of hard work. As soon as the holiday season has concluded, however, their work begins again. February and March are the months in which many trees are culled, which means the small, scrawny trees—that would not have been possible to sell—are disposed of. The winter months are also devoted to equipment repair and property maintenance.

GROWING IN THE INDUSTRY

You don't need to get an advanced degree to learn how to plant, cultivate, and sell Christmas trees. Business skills are essential but can be learned through experience in the field. Getting an entry-level job and working at a nursery or farm can give you some excellent experience. Your best bet is to contact one of the state chapters of the NCTA to request more information and to find out about joining. The NCTA can also help you get in touch with a farmer who can answer your questions.

CHAPTER 9

FIREFIGHTING IN THE WILDERNESS

Wildfires can be devastating, taking human lives and destroying precious natural beauty. Even with advanced technology and techniques, it's never easy to stop a fire. That's why becoming a wildland firefighter is both extremely difficult and extremely important. These brave individuals work shifts of up to 20 hours, ready to spring into action at a moment's notice. Fire seasons—or times when wildfire risks are at their highest—can last for six months, depending on location. During this time, firefighters are isolated from their families and communities, often living in remote locations so they're closer to potential fire areas. Though they make tough sacrifices and put their lives on the line every time they set out into the wilderness to control a fire, most wildland firefighters love their jobs. They are able to use their skills to protect not only people and manmade structures, but also animals and natural beauty.

Unlike most fires that happen in urban areas, wildfires have nearly unlimited fuel and can burn for days and weeks before they're contained.

PROTECTING THE WILDS

Wildland firefighters have a tough job. They're responsible for managing the huge, powerful flames that can engulf hundreds of acres of forest in a matter of hours. There are several different positions within the category of wildland firefighting, ranging from fire spotters (firefighters posted in lookout tow-

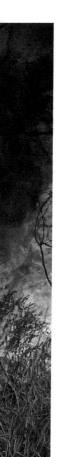

ers) to hotshots and smokejumpers. Professionals, including timber managers and biologists, round out the team. The positions all share some common requirements, including the ability to hike across long distances carrying heavy equipment on one's back. Wildland firefighters have to follow fires into some very remote places, sometimes for weeks on end. Of course, this is all in addition to actually fighting the fires they identify and track down.

Hotshots, an elite crew of firefighters working for the U.S. Forest Service, work in crews of 20 men and women who live and train together. These groups are often called upon to travel wherever they are needed. They specialize in situations in which wildfires begin to threaten urban and suburban areas. Because of their experience and talent, hotshots are generally given the assignment to tackle the toughest part of a fire.

Smokejumpers are firefighters brave enough to parachute into burning forests to fight blazes there. They're flown and airdropped into the extremely remote areas that hotshot crews and other firefighters can't reach. They jump in groups of 2 to 10 people, with each person carrying up to 100 pounds (45 kg) of equipment on their back, and fight the fire for multiple days. When finished, they gather up their equipment and hike to the nearest access road, which is often many miles away. Smokejumpers are chosen from the ranks of experienced firefighters from the NPS, the Forest Service, the Bureau of Land Management, or state forest fire departments. They often

PREVENTING A FIRE USING . . . FIRE?

Firefighting is a tough and sometimes confusing task. For example: did you know that wildland firefighters sometimes must start fires as well as put them out?

Fires are a natural and necessary part of nature. In fact, a forest's health requires the occasional fire. A natural fire—such as one caused by a lightning strike—can clear away old, dead growth and make room for younger, healthier trees. The ash that results from a fire is rich in nutrients and acts as a natural fertilizer as well. However, in modern times, government policies have generally demanded that fires not be allowed to

Modern wildfires are highly dangerous, so setting off smaller blazes before they get out of hand is a smart strategy.

burn. According to the NPS, this has resulted in a heavy buildup of dead vegetation, dense stands of trees, shifts to species that have not evolved and adapted to fire, and even an increase in nonnative fire-prone plants.

Because of these conditions, today's fires tend to be larger, burn hotter, and spread farther and faster. This means they're more severe, more dangerous, and more costly in human, economic, and ecological terms. As a result, controlled burns are now part of national forest policy. By targeting a specific area and starting a fire—which is put out before it spreads beyond that area— firefighters help reduce flammable materials in the forest and help restore the ecosystem to health. Wilderness firefighters sometimes also thin forests: they cut away dead limbs with chain saws, clear dead trees, and pile up and burn any wood that could pose a fire hazard.

have experience as farmers, park rangers, or ranchers, in addition to being accomplished firefighters. Aspiring smokejumpers must be physically fit, and they must successfully complete a boot camp–style training session. Smokejumpers receive good pay— due to the danger of their job—but it's the natural scenery, adventure, and strong sense of teamwork that keeps them serving year after year.

BRAVERY REQUIRED

Federal and state fire management agencies are often on the lookout for temporary firefighters, so experiencing a seasonal workload is a good way to get started in this career. A regional or local forest supervisor often looks to the state employment office for recruiting, so inquire there first. State offices typically begin accepting applications for the upcoming year starting in February. If a state office refers you to the forest supervisor, you will be considered for employment on a crew.

You must be knowledgeable in basic first aid and CPR before you even inquire about one of these high-risk positions. You should also be in excellent physical health and proficient in various outdoor skills, such as using a compass, tying knots, and operating a chain saw.

Entry-level positions can be difficult to land in this field. One possible career path is to start out as a forestry aide or technician before working toward becoming a firefighter. Consider these lower-level positions as a kind of internship. These jobs can consist of challenging work, but they're an excellent introduction to the world of wildland firefighting. Firefighters who are employed by state and national parks aren't required to have college degrees, but a high school diploma is typically necessary. As you move to higher and higher positions, you will be expected to undergo more and more difficult training. Some of this takes place on the job, but you may need to take a course for additional certification.

CHAPTER 10

CAPTURING NATURE DIGITALLY

The best way to appreciate nature is to go out and experience it. The second-best way is to see it through photographs and videos. Nature photographers are responsible for bringing the wild world—which many people will never get to see in person—to magazines and websites for people to enjoy. Starting out as a photographer can be easy—all you really need is a camera. Equally important for the job is patience: most animals won't be like human models, ready and waiting for your arrival in their natural habitat, posing for artistic shots. You'll have to spend hours, days, weeks, or months waiting for rare species to show themselves, and you must be ready to capture the perfect image at a moment's notice. The final requirement for a good photographer is passion—after all, photography is an art form, and you must be dedicated to the craft if you wish to succeed.

HOLD YOUR BREATH, TAKE THE SHOT

Not everyone can land a job with major national organizations, such as National Geographic or the Nature Conservancy, but there are plenty of good opportunities for photographers who want to focus their lens on the natural world. Some photographers obtain full-time work as staff photographers or photo editors at smaller magazines or digital publications. However, most nature photographers work on a freelance basis. Freelance work is less steady and reliable, but it's a good option for photographers still building up a portfolio. Freelance rates vary from client to client.

When you're first starting out as a photographer, it's important to keep your eyes open for opportunities, as they can come from unexpected sources. Many businesses, such as outdoor sporting goods and gardening companies, need photographers to

Photography is a powerful art form, and nature photography helps people appreciate the wild world.

help make their promotional materials—including catalogs, websites, posters, and displays—look good. The greeting card and calendar industries are also possible markets for your images.

Nature photographers must be passionate about nature and motivated to learn about the subjects they photograph. They must master composition,

Though it may seem like you need a lot of equipment to become a photographer, all you need to start out is an eye for nature and a desire to succeed.

or the art of framing a photograph. They must have a healthy curiosity about the technical aspects of photography. A lot more goes into an incredible photograph than just pointing and shooting, so a young photographer has to learn all they can about their cameras and other equipment. Ultimately, professional photographers invest a lot of money in expen-

sive photography gear. They also invest a lot of time in learning how to use it properly.

Nature photography involves a lot of determination, adventurousness, and patience. You may have to wait for hours for the clouds to clear, the sun to reach just the right part of the sky, or a certain animal to pass before your lens. Sometimes, the light will be too harsh or too subdued; sometimes, animals will not stay still for your camera—or maybe they won't appear to you at all. You'll have to learn to cope with these frustrations. Nature photographers must also learn and follow the nature photographer's code of ethics.

DEVELOP YOUR PORTFOLIO

You don't need an advanced art degree to get your photography career started. Beginner and intermediate photography classes are often offered at community centers, arts centers, community colleges,

ART, ETHICALLY

The art of a nature photographer introduces the public to incredible wild animals and natural habitats they might never see otherwise. Therefore, it's important that photographers always work to protect the wildlife they are documenting. Here are a few principles in the nature photographer's professional code of ethics:

- Humans should rarely appear in nature photographs.
- It's important that viewers are able to trust a nature photographer's work. Photographs that are manipulated in any way—by computer editing or airbrushing, for example—are not considered to be true nature photography.
- Learn about the behavior and ecology of your animal subjects before photographing them. Don't interfere with animals' natural behaviors. Respect the routines of animals. Don't approach nests or dens too closely. Never directly interact with any baby animal. If an animal seems agitated, back away and try to take a picture from a distance.
- Don't disturb wild creatures by playing loud music, littering, or driving recklessly or off approved roads.
- It's acceptable to transport insects and reptiles from their habitat to a studio for photographing, as long as they're returned as soon as possible. Permission to do so from the proper authorities must be granted.
- It's never acceptable to injure or kill an animal for the purpose of photography.
- Nocturnal creatures should be photographed in the early morning or late afternoon when they are less active but awake. This will make

it easier for you to get the shot, and you won't be disrupting their natural behavior.

- Don't trample grasslands, marshes, and wild-flower patches when photographing plants and flowers. Damage to these plants and flowers affects all species in the ecosystem. Stay on designated trails. Wildflowers should never be picked.
- Inform the appropriate authorities or land-owners of your presence and purpose. Also inform them about anyone who is engaging in inappropriate behavior.

universities, and independent workshops across the country. It's a good idea to get a strong foundation in the artistic and technical aspects of photography before trying to make it your profession. Though it's possible to learn by simply going out and taking pictures, participating in a class that teaches you the basics will significantly speed up your growth as an artist.

Before getting out in the wilds, spend as much time as possible researching the species you plan to photograph. Learning about their habitats will help you actually locate them—finding wild animals isn't as easy as it sounds! Assign yourself smaller projects as you go, and make every picture a learning opportunity. Buy a nature magazine you like and study it. Look up its submission guidelines to learn how freelancers can get in touch with the publisher.

The North American Nature Photography Association (NANPA) sponsors a student scholarship program that can be a young photographer's dream come true. Ten high school students are selected annually to attend a five-day seminar in the Great Smoky Mountains National Park. The winners of this scholarship are given the opportunity to learn more about ecology and wildlife, participate in special field workshops, and receive photographic instruction from nature photography and publishing professionals.

NANPA also offers many smaller scholarships and grants to budding photographers, and many other organizations do too. Search around for information on learning opportunities with local or regional groups—you may be surprised how many like-minded individuals are exploring and taking pictures of nature nearby.

CHAPTER 11

THE ECOTOURISM ECONOMY

Natural beauty exists everywhere in the world, but there are certain locations that are able to truly take one's breath away. As more and more people become interested in seeing these locations firsthand, businesses crop up to help make that easier. This is how the ecotourism industry was born. Ecotourism refers to people traveling to isolated, exotic areas—like the Amazon rain forest, Australian outback, or Arctic Circle—to experience nature at its finest. Hotels in these locations are often called ecolodges, and most try to minimize the impact their business will have on the local area. Many ecolodges also offer programs and packages that support and maintain native communities nearby. As this industry continues to expand over the coming decades, there will be increased demand and opportunity for nature lovers to get involved and start up a career bringing others to see natural beauty in faraway places.

PLANNING ECO TRIPS

To be successful as a member of the ecotourism industry, a person needs good people skills, the ability to work independently and creatively, and a sense of adventure. Although you don't need to go to college to be qualified, you need to be willing to do lots of your own research, both by reading and by visiting the places where you someday wish to lead tours. Once you have laid the groundwork, you can begin guiding ecotours for an established and reputable ecotour operator—or even start your own company.

As an ecotravel guide or tour group leader, you must develop an understanding of—and a respect for—the complex ecosystems of plants, animals, and humans in your

Ecotourists want to experience the natural world. As a guide, you have to make sure they have a good time—and do so responsibly, without disturbing the ecosystem.

SEARCHING FOR UNIQUE EXPERIENCES

There are unique and fascinating ecotourism locations all over the world. Here are just a few popular ecotourism destinations:

- **Kapawi Ecolodge, Ecuador:** Guests reach Kapawi Lodge by taking a small plane deep into the heart of the Amazon rain forest. At the lodge, tourists stay in solar-powered cabins built by indigenous local craftsmen. The resort carefully minimizes its impact on the surrounding jungle out of respect for nature. Guests can kayak the river, hike in the jungle, or visit a traditional Achuar village, where they may learn about everyday chores or take part in a traditional dream interpretation ceremony.

- **Tassia Lodge, Kenya:** Located atop a rocky bluff overlooking a gorgeous valley teeming with wildlife, this ecolodge participates in local environmental projects to protect trees and prevent soil erosion. Guests can take a safari on foot through the bush, observing animals like zebras and elephants in their natural habitat. The Tassia also offers opportunities to learn how to throw a spear or use a traditional bow with a Maasai warrior, visit a local traditional village, or even go on expeditions across the valley.

- **Daintree Ecolodge, Australia:** Guests of this Australian resort stay in a tree house perched above or among the trees of the Daintree rain forest. Guests can explore the local ecosystems, including the forest, the shoreline, and the nearby Great Barrier Reef. The lodge has close ties to local Aboriginal communities. Tourists may also participate in Aboriginal culture by going on guided "walkabouts," learning traditional skills, or taking an art and cultural workshop.

As the ecotourism industry grows, more and more ecolodges like this will open to the public, allowing people from all over the world to enjoy unique natural habitats.

natural surroundings, wherever they may be. As a guide, you must be knowledgeable and entertaining, able to communicate important science and history in the form of accessible and interesting talks. You should try to involve local people as much as possible in your tours and encourage your clients to support local businesses. In doing so, the preservation of the environment will economically benefit local residents, and your travelers will learn about the culture of their hosts.

If you do go on to own your own touring business, you should try to fill as many positions as possible with local employees. Many ecotours operate in places where there are limited job opportunities for locals.

Above all, you should avoid and minimize any environmental harm to fragile ecosystems and encourage your travelers to get involved in conservation efforts, both locally and at home.

GETTING A FOOT IN THE DOOR

There are many skills that contribute to the success of an ecotourism professional, but perhaps the most important among them are safety, communication, and an understanding of the natural world. With just a high school degree, you should be able to break into the industry and acquire on-the-job training and experience. If you want to work your way up, it will likely be necessary for you to take some specialized courses or participate in company-led training seminars, but you will probably not need a college degree.

The International Ecotourism Society (TIES) offers training in this field in the form of forums, field seminars, and workshops. Park rangers, landscape architects, and other nature professionals from dozens of countries around the globe attend the organization's events, which makes them a great opportunity to network with other members of the industry. By getting your name out there, you'll improve your chances of finding long-term employment with an established company or even developing a customer base for your own business.

animal husbandry The study and practice of breeding and raising livestock.

boatswain A supervisor of a boat's deckhands who is also responsible for repairing fishing gear, boat equipment, and nets.

cattle drive The movement of large herds of cattle from one place to another, often guided by wranglers on horseback.

composting Creating a mixture of decaying organic substances, such as vegetable scraps and dead leaves.

conservation The act of preserving and protecting a natural resource, ecosystem, or imperiled plant or animal.

ecosystem A system made up of a community of living organisms interacting with their physical environment.

ecotourism Environmentally sensitive travel in exotic, often fragile, natural environments, especially to observe wildlife, support conservation efforts, and sustain the livelihoods of the local people.

ethics The rules of conduct governing an individual or group.

fire spotter A ranger posted in a lookout tower that alerts firefighters when a forest fire breaks out.

fish processing The transformation of fish from a wild catch to a product ready for market.

horticulture The science and art of growing fruits, vegetables, flowers, or plants.

hotshot Elite U.S. Forest Service firefighter who specializes in forest fires that threaten urban and suburban communities.

internship A program that allows someone to receive supervised practical experience in a field of work.

naturalist An expert in natural history, especially the study of plants and animals in their natural surroundings.

outfitter A company that offers tour packages, such as white-water rafting excursions.

pruning Trimming a tree's branches to control its growth and shape and to prevent pest infestations.

seedling A very small, young tree.

smokejumper A person who parachutes into remote areas to fight forest fires that other firefighters can't reach.

urban farm A farm that grows produce and sometimes livestock and poultry in an urban environment. Urban farms can be found in former vacant lots, in abandoned buildings, and on rooftops.

wrangler A ranch hand that takes care of horses and other livestock.

American Community Gardening Association

3271 Main Street
College Park, GA 30337
(877) 275-2242
Website: communitygarden.org
Facebook: @AmericanCommunityGarden
   Association
Instagram: @communitygardeningacga
Twitter: @ACGA_CommGarden

This growing organization includes both professional and volunteer gardeners. It supports community gardening efforts all across the United States.

American Whitewater

P.O. Box 1540
Cullowhee, NC 28723
(828) 586-1930
Website: bcguestranches.com
Facebook and Instagram: @AmericanWhitewater
Twitter: @AmerWhitewater

This conservation organization is committed to restoring and maintaining white-water rivers all across the United States.

BC Guest Ranchers Association

(877) 278-2922
Website: bcguestranches.com
Facebook: @BCGuestRanchers

Founded in 1985, this professional organization for dude ranch owners helps members—who must meet strict requirements—connect with guests, learn more about the industry, and grow to reach their full potential.

Fisheries and Oceans Canada
200 Kent Street, Station 13E228
Ottawa, ON K1A 0E6
Canada
(613) 993-0999
Website: https://www.dfo-mpo.gc.ca/index
   -eng.htm
Facebook: @FisheriesOceansCanada
Instagram: @fisheriesoceanscan
This Canadian government agency works with public and private employees and organizations to monitor, regulate, and protect the country's fishing areas and waterways.

National Park Service (NPS)
1849 C Street NW
Washington, DC 20240
(202) 208-6843
Website: http://nps.gov
Facebook and Instagram: @nationalparkservice
Twitter: @NatlParkService
This government agency is responsible for protecting and maintaining the entire park system of the United States. The NPS runs volunteer and professional training programs for people who love the great outdoors.

FOR FURTHER READING

Faulkner, Nicholas, and Janey Levy. *Conservation and You*. New York, NY: Rosen Central, 2019.

Hand, Carol. *Urban Gardening*. Minneapolis, MN: Lerner Publications, 2016.

Kallen, Stuart A. *Careers If You Like the Outdoors*. San Diego, CA: ReferencePoint Press, 2018.

Labrecque, Ellen. *Land Trusts and National Parks*. Ann Arbor, MI: Cherry Lake Publishing, 2018.

Palmer, Andrea. *We're Going Freshwater Fishing*. New York, NY: PowerKids Press, 2017.

Siber, Kate, and Chris Turnham. *National Parks of the U.S.A.* Minneapolis, MN: Wide Eyed Editions, 2018.

Wilhelmi, Christy. *Gardening for Geeks: All the Science You Need for Successful Organic Gardening*. Mount Joy, PA: Fox Chapel Publishers, 2020.

Young, Karen Romano. *Whale Quest: Working Together to Save Endangered Species*. Minneapolis, MN: Twenty-First Century Books, 2017.

ABOUT THE AUTHOR

Siyavush Saidian lives with his wife and two corgis in New York. A lover of books and writing, he knew college was the right path for him, but he realizes that's not the case for everyone. He's excited to help young people find jobs they love, just like he did.

CREDITS